You Are Part Of An Epic Team

www.ingramcontent.com/pod-product-compliance
Lightning Source LLC
Chambersburg PA
CBHW070433220526
45466CB00004B/1651
9781660852796